DATE DUE			
DEC 29 04			

6/00

JACKSON COUNTY
Library Services

HEADQUARTERS
413 West Main Street
Medford, Oregon 97501

Festivals of the World

COSTA RICA

Gareth Stevens Publishing
MILWAUKEE

Written by
FREDERICK FISHER

Edited by
GERALDINE MESENAS

Designed by
LOO CHUAN MING

Picture research by
SUSAN JANE MANUEL

First published in North America in 1999 by
Gareth Stevens Publishing
1555 North RiverCenter Drive, Suite 201
Milwaukee, Wisconsin 53212 USA

For a free color catalog describing Gareth
Stevens' list of high-quality books and multimedia
programs, call
1-800-542-2595 (USA)
or 1-800-461-9120 (Canada).
Gareth Stevens Publishing's Fax: (414) 225-0377.
See our catalog, too, on the World Wide Web:
http://gsinc.com

© TIMES EDITIONS PTE LTD 1999
Originated and designed by
Times Books International
an imprint of Times Editions Pte Ltd
Times Centre, 1 New Industrial Road
Singapore 536196
Printed in Singapore

Library of Congress Cataloging-in-Publication Data:
Fisher, Frederick.
Costa Rica / by Frederick Fisher.
p. cm.—(Festivals of the world)
Includes bibliographical references and index.
Summary: Describes how the culture of Costa Rica
is reflected in its many festivals, including Día del
Boyero, Semana Santa, and Día de las Culturas.
ISBN 0-8368-2022-3 (lib. bdg.)
1. Festivals—Costa Rica—Juvenile literature.
2. Costa Rica—Social life and customs—Juvenile
literature. [1. Festivals—Costa Rica. 2. Holidays—
Costa Rica. 3. Costa Rica—Social life and
customs.] I. Title. II. Series.
GT4817.A2F57   1999
394.2697286—dc21   98-31421

1 2 3 4 5 6 7 8 9 03 02 01 00 99

CONTENTS

It's Festival Time . . .

Ticos can have a party for almost any reason. The Costa Rican festival, or *fiesta* [fee-YES-ta], is an elaborate event and sometimes lasts for a week! There are horse shows, parades, and bullfights. Beauty contests, carousels, fireworks, and athletic events are the heart of the festivities. Special holiday foods complete the Costa Rican fiesta. So, come on and join in the fun. It's festival time in Costa Rica!

WHERE'S COSTA RICA?

Costa Rica is a small, beautiful country on the **isthmus** of Central America. It connects Panama and Nicaragua and is sandwiched between the Pacific Ocean and the Caribbean Sea. Costa Rica is best known for its tropical rain forests and its numerous plant and animal species. In Spanish, *Costa Rica* means "rich coast," and it is indeed rich in coastline.

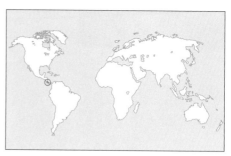

A beautiful Costa Rican girl with a juicy mango.

Who are the Ticos?

Costa Ricans are called Ticos because of their unique way of speaking Spanish. They often replace the Spanish diminutive, *tito*, with *tico*.

Many races of people live in Costa Rica. Hidalgos are descendants of the Spaniards that came with Columbus. Many Spaniards married the native Indians. Their offspring make up the largest ethnic group in Costa Rica, the mestizos. Smaller groups include the Africans, or cacaos, and the Chinese, or chinos.

Over the years, these groups of people have interacted well and prospered. Today, Costa Rica is a beautiful, peaceful, democratic society.

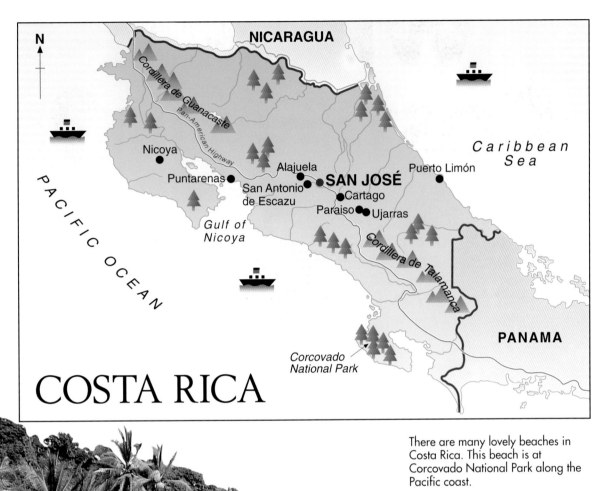

COSTA RICA

NICARAGUA

N

Cordillera de Guanacaste

Pan-American Highway

Caribbean Sea

Nicoya

Puntarenas

Alajuela

San Antonio de Escazu

SAN JOSÉ

Puerto Limón

Cartago

Paraiso

Ujarras

PACIFIC OCEAN

Gulf of Nicoya

Cordillera de Talamanca

PANAMA

Corcovado National Park

There are many lovely beaches in Costa Rica. This beach is at Corcovado National Park along the Pacific coast.

When's the Fiesta?

SPRING

- ✪ **ANNUAL ORCHID SHOW**
- ✪ **SAN JOSÉ DAY**—On March 19th, Costa Ricans living in or near San José celebrate with cattle shows, rodeos, bullfights, and horse races.
- ✪ **DÍA DEL BOYERO**
- ✪ **SEMANA SANTA**
  - ✪ **EASTER**
  - ✪ **DÍA DE JUAN SANTAMARIA**
  - ✪ **PILGRIMAGE OF THE VIRGIN OF THE RESCUE**— On the third Sunday of April, thousands of people walk from Paraiso to Ujarras and back to honor the first patron saint of Costa Rica.

Ticos love to dance. See other colorful dancers in Costa Rica's many fiestas!

SUMMER

- ✪ **FIESTA DE LOS MANGOS (MANGO FESTIVAL)**—Celebrated in late June in Alajuela Central Park, this fiesta is nine days of nonstop activities, from folk music and crafts, to parades, floats, and farmers' markets.
- ✪ **VIRGEN DEL MAR (VIRGIN OF THE SEA)**—A procession of fishing boats and big yachts sails through the Gulf of Nicoya at Puntarenas. A carnival follows in the second week of July.
  - ✪ **VIRGEN DE LOS ANGELES**
  - ✪ **LA ASSUNCION DE LA MADRE (MOTHER'S DAY)**

AUTUMN

- ✪ **DESFILE DE FAROLES (MARCH OF THE LANTERNS)**—On the eve of Independence Day, children celebrate in schools with many activities, ending the day with a colorful march of handmade lanterns.
- ✪ **DÍA DE LA INDEPENDENCIA NACIONAL (INDEPENDENCE DAY)**—On September 15th, Ticos celebrate their freedom from Spain in 1821.
- ✪ **DÍA DE LAS CULTURAS (COLUMBUS DAY) AND CARNEVALES DE LIMÓN (LIMÓN CARNIVAL)**

Join us as we dance to the Caribbean beat at the Limón Carnival on pages 12-15!

WINTER

- ✪ **FEAST OF THE IMMACULATE CONCEPTION (HOLY COMMUNION DAY)**—Celebrated on December 8th.
- ✪ **FIESTA DE LA YEGUITA (THE LITTLE MARE)**—Celebrated in Nicoya on December 12th. The statue of the Virgin of Guadalupe is carried in a procession. Fireworks, bullfights, and concerts add to the excitement.
- ✪ **CHRISTMAS** ✪ **NEW YEAR**
- ✪ **FIESTA DEL FIN DEL ANO (END OF THE YEAR)**—This fiesta is celebrated from Christmas through January 2nd.
- ✪ **EL JUEGO DE LOS DIABILITOS (GAME OF THE LITTLE DEVILS)**—Indians wear masks and act out a battle with the Spanish conquistadors.
- ✪ **ALEJUELITA**—This celebration on January 15th honors the Black Christ of Esquipulas. On this day, many people climb a 6,200-foot (1,890-meter) mountain to visit a cross at the top.

CELEBRATING INDEPENDENCE

I ndependence Day and Juan Santamaria Day remind Ticos of the importance of independence. Costa Rica gained independence from Spain on September 15, 1821, after three centuries of colonial rule. This special event is commemorated in colorful, annual parades all over the country.

On Juan Santamaria Day, Ticos remember the courage of an 11-year-old boy named Juan Santamaria, and they celebrate with an exciting carnival and fair. Read on to find out more about these important days!

Schoolchildren await the start of the Independence Day parade, wearing hats in the three colors of the Costa Rican flag.

Independence Day

At precisely six o'clock in the evening on September 14th, all traffic in the capital city of San José and other parts of Costa Rica stops. It is an amazing sight, as cars, buses, trucks, motorcycles, and other vehicles all stop where they are along the roads. People all over Costa Rica stop what they are doing and sing the national anthem.

On September 15th, all Ticos celebrate Independence Day. It is a national holiday. Parades highlight the festivities, and schoolchildren are the main participants. On Independence Day, the red, white, and blue Costa Rican flag flies proudly everywhere.

On Independence Day, children are all smiles as they carry their national flag with pride.

9

Above: Schoolchildren perform a traditional dance on Children's Day. Don't they look wonderful in their colorful costumes?

Below: In the March of the Lanterns, young children proudly show off colorful lanterns they make themselves. On the eve of Independence Day, the streets glow with the light from hundreds of colorful handmade lanterns. It's a truly beautiful sight!

Children's Day

Many events, especially for Costa Rican children, are held in preparation for Independence Day. On September 9th, for example, all schools celebrate Children's Day. There are no classes on this day. Instead, teachers prepare many exciting activities for the children. The highlights of the day are the dances and plays performed by schoolchildren.

The March of the Lanterns

On the eve of Independence Day (September 14th), children play a special part in a lantern parade, called the March of the Lanterns. At night, families gather in the streets and in parks, and children carry colorful handmade lanterns in little processions throughout the cities.

Juan Santamaria

Juan was a **mulatto** boy from Alajuela. He was a drummer boy in the army. In 1856, the Costa Ricans waged a war against the troops of self-proclaimed ruler William Walker in the town of Rivas. In this battle, Juan showed great courage when he carried a torch through deadly battle lines and set fire to enemy buildings. Through Juan's brave efforts, the tide of the battle turned in Costa Rica's favor. Unfortunately, Juan lost his life in that battle. He was only 11 years old. Juan Santamaria has since become a national hero and a symbol of bravery and **patriotism**.

This monument in Alajuela is dedicated to Costa Rica's national hero, Juan Santamaria.

The Hedgehog Fair and Carnival

Día de Juan Santamaria [dee-ah day WAN sahn-tah-MAHR-ee-ah], or Juan Santamaria Day, is celebrated on April 11th with a fair and a carnival in Alajuela. The Hedgehog Fair, named for Juan's nickname "The Hedgehog", is organized by the Red Cross to raise funds for the needy. The carnival has horse parades and musical concerts, and wonderful food smells fill the air. There is an amusement park, too, with thrilling rides for all to enjoy. Children especially love this carnival as they get a whole week off school, but it is a favorite time for all Ticos, children and adults alike.

Think about this

Most countries commemorate their independence from a foreign power with a national holiday and celebrate with parades and other exciting activities. Is Independence Day a national holiday in your country? What are your favorite ways to celebrate it?

DÍA DE LAS CULTURAS

Ticos love carnivals and parades. They look forward to the music, dancing, and special foods that are always part of these festivities. The biggest carnival of the year is held in Costa Rica's Atlantic port, Puerto Limón. This carnival commemorates Christopher Columbus's arrival in Costa Rica on September 18, 1502. During the carnival, the streets of Limón are filled with revelers in brightly colored costumes dancing to the rhythmic drum beats of Caribbean music.

Opposite: Costa Ricans dress up in the most beautiful and outrageous outfits during the Limón Carnival. It is, after all, the biggest party of the year!

Below: These schoolgirls are performing a lively, colorful dance. Schoolchildren prepare for carnival performances months in advance.

Celebrating Christopher Columbus's arrival

Columbus Day, or *Día de las Culturas* [DEE-ah day lahs cool-TOO-rahs], which means "Day of the Cultures," is a week-long celebration of Columbus's arrival at the port of Limón during his fourth and last voyage to the Americas.

Ticos and visitors alike gather at Limón each year to celebrate this historic occasion. The highlight of the week is the parade, a procession of hundreds of people dressed in wild and colorful costumes. Dancers perform for hours as everyone claps along to the beat of the music. The performers, however, are not the only people dancing. Before long, many onlookers—children, adults, and tourists—are on their feet, moving to the exciting, foot-tapping music of the Caribbean!

Keep to the Caribbean beat with these young **percussionists**!

A Caribbean boys band provides rhythmic music for the parade.

The party goes on and on

Throughout Carnival week, the quiet port city of Limón changes **dramatically**. It becomes a big party that lasts day and night. The drumbeat rhythms of Caribbean music echo through the city streets. The music never stops, and the people never seem to sleep.

Limón's many restaurants stay open 24 hours a day during the Carnival. Food and drink stands all over Limón dish out delicious *tamales* [tah-MAH-lays], a popular Costa Rican snack, and tall, cold drinks at all hours of the day.

Many other activities take place during Carnival week. One of the most popular activities is a beauty contest to elect a Carnival Queen. Costa Rican-style bullfights are also popular, as are water sports competitions held on the beautiful beaches north of Limón.

Think about this
When Columbus landed at Limón in 1502, the country was inhabited by local Indians, who greeted Columbus with gifts of gold. Today, these native people make up less than one percent of Costa Rica's entire population.

A contestant in Limón's Carnival Queen contest.

15

DÍA DEL BOYERO

In Costa Rica, the oxcart, or *carreta* [ka-REH-tah], is a national symbol. On the second Sunday in March, over 100 oxcart drivers, or *boyeros* [boy-AIR-ohs], from all over the country gather at San Antonio de Escazu to celebrate *Día del Boyero* [DEE-ah del boy-AIR-oh], or Oxcart Driver's Day. It is a wonderful event, with crowds of people lining the streets to watch colorful oxcart parades.

People, boyeros, and oxcarts fill the church in San Antonio de Escazu as a priest blesses each oxcart in the parade.

Although oxcarts are not used as much as they once were, they are an enduring Costa Rican symbol. Beautifully painted oxcarts have become a folk art form in Costa Rica today.

Join the parade

In the morning, a long line of oxcarts assembles outside the city center. Oxen are hitched up to the carts, two oxen harnessed at the front of each cart, one on each side of a long T-shaped bar, or yoke. On Día del Boyero, even the oxen are dressed up! Fancy leather headdresses with bells are attached over the oxen's curved horns and down their noses. The bells ring as the oxen walk, making a delightful bell symphony.

The center of the day's festivities is the church, where a priest, dressed in his fanciest robes, overlooks the parade and blesses each oxcart as it passes by. At the parade, everyone is in high spirits, waving, cheering, and throwing confetti. Local bands play music on stringed instruments, called *cimarronas* [sim-ah-ROHN-ahs], as young people dance to traditional melodies. Throughout the day, everyone snacks on maize, rice, potatoes, and meat and has a wonderful time!

A line of boyeros with their oxcarts and oxen wait patiently for the parade to start.

Above: The oxcart was an important form of transportation in the 19th century and was used to transport coffee, one of Costa Rica's most important crops.

The history of the oxcart

Oxcarts were very important to the Costa Rican economy in the 19th century. In the 1840s, coffee was a major export crop, and oxcarts were used to transport the coffee from the fields, over the mountains, and to the seaport for shipping to other countries. The oxcarts had to be sturdy enough to carry 800 to 1,000 pounds (360 to 450 kilograms) each. Wheels are a vital part of the oxcart. Roads become very muddy during the rainy season, so oxcart wheels are made with 16 wedges of wood held together by an iron rim. Mud slides off the solid faces of these wheels.

Costa Rica's cowboys are part of the Día del Boyero festivities.

Oxcart folk art

Oxcart painting is one of the best known examples of Costa Rican folk art. It is not clear how oxcart painting began, but one story says it was started by the wife of a cartmaker who was attracted by the solid surfaces of the wheels and started painting designs on them and on the rest of the cart. Before long, farmers started painting their oxcarts. Many of them took tremendous pride in their work. Oxcarts are painted in bright colors, usually red, with beautiful blue and yellow designs.

Today, oxcart painters are celebrated artists in Costa Rica, and old painted oxcarts have become valuable collectors' items. The old carts are kept in good condition for the annual boyero parade. Many new carts are made every year, and the artists still take great pride in their work. Each design is carefully painted on. Some artists spend months painting one oxcart.

Oxcart painters sometimes take many months to complete the beautiful and intricate designs.

Think about this

San Antonio de Escazu is the center of oxcart production, and making decorative oxcarts is big business. Not all decorative oxcarts, however, are used in parades. Smaller oxcarts are used as serving carts for parties, and many Costa Rican restaurants use them to serve food and drink. **Miniature** versions are normally bought as souvenirs for friends, or as toys for children.

SEMANA SANTA

Maundy Thursday and Good Friday are official national holidays in Costa Rica. Catholics all over the country celebrate with great **enthusiasm**. Most companies and offices are closed, and processions are held in all the towns. The most beautiful processions are held in larger cities, such as Cartago. The highlight of the holiday is the reenactment of the Passage of Christ.

The Passage of Christ is reenacted with amateur actors playing the roles. It is a heartrending performance.

Viernes Santo

Good Friday, called *Viernes Santo* [vee-AIR-ness SAHN-toh], is a solemn day when Catholics mourn Christ's crucifixion. Everyone wears black for a morning mass in church. A sermon, delivered before noon, is followed by a street procession reenacting the Passage of Christ.

The Passage of Christ

The Passage of Christ reenacts the events that occurred on Jesus' journey to Calvary, where he was crucified. An actor playing the role of Jesus carries a large wooden cross through the streets, surrounded by actors playing Roman soldiers. Large crowds gather to watch this heartrending performance.

Along the way, other actors join in the procession, performing the roles of Mary Magdalene, who washed Jesus' feet; Veronica, who wiped his face; a Samaritan woman, who offered water to Jesus; the Virgin Mary; and the apostle John.

At a chosen site, the actor in the role of Jesus is "nailed" to the cross, and the crowd is silent with grief. For thousands of years, this procession has been repeated annually to remind all Catholics of Christ's sacrifice.

A large street audience solemnly watches as an actor playing the role of Jesus reenacts Christ's difficult journey to Calvary.

The majority of Costa Ricans are Roman Catholics, and they celebrate religious festivities with great fervor.

The Good Friday procession

At the end of the procession, the actor portraying Jesus is taken down from the cross and laid on a gold sepulcher, which is a special platform or stand. A group of one hundred men, all wearing black suits, carry the sepulcher to church. They are followed by Catholic priests and actors playing the roles of the Virgin Mary and the apostle John, both dressed in black. A band plays mournful music as all the other characters follow the sepulcher into the church.

Children play a special part in this procession. Several young girls, two to six years old, dress as little angels and are taken into church sitting or standing on small platforms carried on men's shoulders. Other young girls in lovely, white dresses and blue scarfs lead the procession into the church.

Judas Day

On the Saturday evening before Easter, the solemnity of Good Friday ends and Easter fun begins. Boys carry the effigy of Judas through the streets and hang it from a tree. According to the bible, Judas, one of Jesus' 12 apostles, **betrayed** Jesus to the Romans for money. After Jesus' crucifixion, Judas was so ashamed of what he had done that he hanged himself from a tree.

On Judas Day, people playfully take others' belongings and put them under the effigy of Judas. As the owners retrieve their belongings, those watching good-naturedly laugh at and ridicule them.

At dawn on Easter Sunday, the effigy of Judas, which is stuffed with fireworks, is burned as people shout and cheer.

Above: The effigy of Judas is hung from a tree on Judas Day. On this day, everyone has fun and plays practical jokes on each other. This tradition was adopted by Ticos to relieve some of the solemnity of Good Friday.

Left: A beautiful little angel, wearing a lovely white and gold dress and feathery wings, walks to the procession grounds with her older sister.

Think about this

Holy Week, or *Semana Santa* [say-MAHN-ah SAHN-tah], is one of the most important events on the Catholic calendar, and Costa Rican Catholics celebrate it with elaborate processions and feasts. What religious events do you and your family celebrate? How do you celebrate them?

VIRGEN DE LOS ANGELES

O n August 2nd, Costa Rica celebrates its very own **miracle** at the Basilica of Our Lady of the Angels in Cartago. This festival honors Costa Rica's patron saint, the *Virgen de Los Angeles* [VAIR-hen day los AHN-hail-ays], or the Virgin of the Angels. On this day, thousands of people from all over Central America make a pilgrimage to Cartago. Some **pilgrims** walk to Cartago from San José and even from as far away as Panama and Nicaragua!

The beautiful shrine of *La Negrita* [la nay-GREE-tah], or Little Black One, in the basilica.

The Basilica of Our Lady of the Angels in Cartago is the center of activity on August 2nd every year.

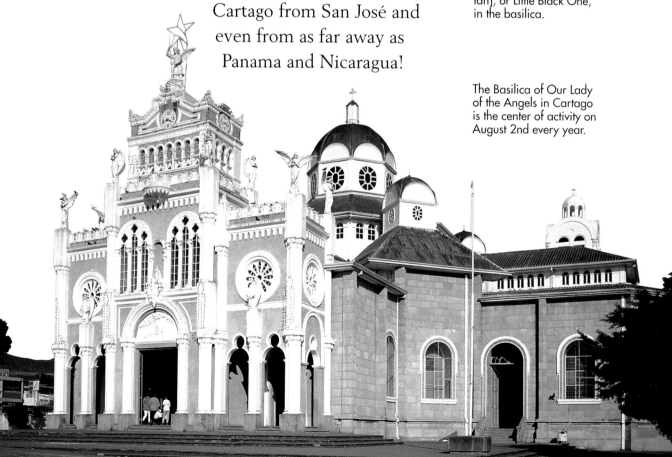

The miracle

On August 2, 1635, a little girl discovered a small, black statue of the Virgin Mary in the woods. She took it home, but it mysteriously returned to its location in the woods. After the same thing happened three times, she took the statue to a priest. Again, the statue returned to the woods.

This event was declared a miracle, and the statue became known as La Negrita, or Little Black One. A beautiful church, the Basilica of Our Lady of the Angels, was later built on the site of La Negrita's appearance to commemorate the miracle.

The procession

The highlight of this festival is the procession of the La Negrita. After a solemn mass, attended by important members of the church and the government, hundreds of people form a beautiful procession carrying La Negrita to Mount Carmel's church in downtown Cartago. Later that day, another procession carries the statue back to its shrine in the Basilica.

La Negrita is believed to possess miraculous healing powers. On August 2nd, people pray to La Negrita to cure their ailments, making **pledges** and promises of thanks if their prayers are answered. The La Negrita shrine is filled with gifts from pilgrims who have been cured.

THINGS FOR YOU TO DO

Before Columbus landed at Puerto Limón in 1502, there were small, scattered groups of native Indians living in Costa Rica. Not very much is known about their culture because they left very little evidence of how they lived. Archaeologists today are attempting to find out more about these ancient cultures through **excavations**.

Pre-Columbian art

Although not much is known about how the ancient peoples of Costa Rica lived, we do know that they were very artistic. Pre-Columbian clay and ceramic figures and pottery have been unearthed at sites where these ancient peoples once lived. Some of these objects date back almost 3,000 years! The figures represent gods, animals, and people. Some are rather bizarre, but others are very beautiful, such as the jade figures held in the National Museum in San José. Read on to find out how to make a pre-Columbian clay figure of your own!

What you will need

You can make a clay figure of any animal or object you want. To make your pre-Columbian clay figure, you will need modeling clay, small beads for the eyes, and a butter knife and some toothpicks for shaping the figure and carving delicate designs on it.

Make a pre-Columbian clay figure

Use this book or another book from your library to find a picture of the person, animal, or object you want your clay figure to represent. Keep the picture in front of you while you make the figure. Wet the modeling clay and mold it into the general form of the figure. Use the butter knife to shape the clay and toothpicks to define the facial features and to etch other small details and intricate designs. Put small beads where the eyes should be. Let the clay figure dry for a few hours, then place it on a table or a shelf to make a wonderful decorative piece.

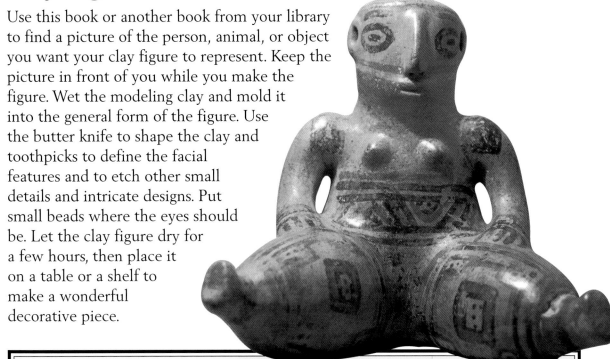

MAKE AN OXCART

T he oxcart is a national symbol of Costa Rica and has become a wonderful art form. Oxcart painters take great pride in their work, often taking many months to complete these colorful art pieces. Follow the simple steps below to make your very own oxcart!

You will need:

1. Brown paper
2. A pencil
3. Paint brushes
4. A round stick or dowel — 8" (20 cm) long
5. 2 flat sticks — 8" (20 cm) and 3" (7.5 cm) in length
6. A shoe box
7. Scissors
8. Glue
9. Tape
10. Tempera paints
11. 4 small styrofoam squares
12. 2 styrofoam discs
13. A paint tray

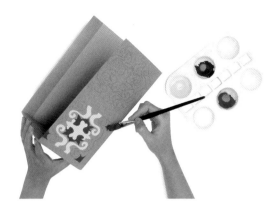

1 Cut off one end of the shoe box. Cover the whole box with brown paper.

2 Draw your favorite designs on the outside of the box, and paint them.

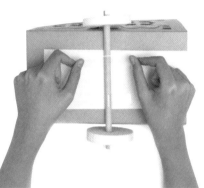

3 Poke the round stick through the styrofoam discs. Position one disc at each end of the stick to make the wheels of the oxcart. Glue a styrofoam square on each side of the protruding ends of the stick to prevent the wheels from coming loose. Attach the stick to the bottom of the box with tape.

4 Glue the short flat stick across the long one to form a cross. Use tape to attach the cross to the bottom of the box at the open end. Now you have your very own Costa Rican oxcart!

MAKE ENSALADA DE FRUTAS

A wide variety of fresh fruits grow in Costa Rica. Ticos enjoy fruits in juices, salads, and desserts. Follow the simple steps below to make *ensalada de frutas* [EN-sah-LAH-dah day FREW-tahs], or fruit salad.

You will need:
1. 8 fl. oz. (240 ml) of warm water
2. A 3-oz. (90-g) package of jello powder
3. A pint (450 g) of ice cream
4. 1 cup (225 g) sliced kiwi fruit
5. 1 cup (225 g) sliced pineapple
6. 1 cup (225 g) sliced strawberries
7. A large spoon
8. A mixing bowl

1 In a mixing bowl, combine the jello powder with warm water. Put the mixture in the refrigerator to cool. Prepare the jello at least one day ahead.

2 Put spoonfuls of sliced kiwi fruit, pineapple, and strawberries into a dessert bowl.

3 Add spoonfuls of solidified jello and mix it with the fruit.

4 Put a scoop of ice cream on top of the fruit and jello mixture. Your ensalada de frutas is ready to be served!

GLOSSARY

betrayed, 23 — Gave information to an enemy of one's country or friends that could harm the country or friends.

dramatically, 15 — Vividly; strikingly.

enthusiasm, 20 — Intense interest.

excavations, 26 — Diggings to uncover objects buried in the ground.

isthmus, 4 — A narrow strip of land between two bodies of water connecting two larger pieces of land.

miniature, 19 — A very small copy or model of something.

miracle, 24 — A wonderful, surprising, and scientifically impossible event thought to be caused by God.

mulatto, 11 — A person who has both a black parent and a white parent.

patriotism, 11 — Love of and loyalty to one's country.

percussionists, 14 — People who make music by beating or striking an instrument, such as a drum.

pilgrims, 24 — People who travel to holy places to honor their religious beliefs.

pledges, 25 — Promises or agreements.

INDEX

Picture credits
A.N.A. Press Agency: 18 (top), 19; DDB Stock Photo: 6, 8, 9, 11, 16 (bottom), 17, 24 (both), 27 (bottom); Dave G. Houser Stock Photography: 5, 26; Jason Lauré: 10 (both); Pietro Scozzari: 1, 3 (both), 7 (bottom), 12, 13, 14 (both), 15, 25, 27 (top); Kay Shaw Photography: 28; David Simson: 23 (top); John Skiffington: 7 (top), 21 (both), 22, 23 (bottom); South American Pictures: 16 (top), 18 (bottom); Topham Picturepoint: 2; Travel Ink: 4, 20

Digital scanning by Superskill Graphics Pte Ltd.

32